OBJECT TALKS
from Sports Kids Love

VERNA KOKMEYER

Standard®
PUBLISHING

Cincinnati, Ohio

DEDICATION

To Nanette, Greg, Craig, and Marissa, with thanks for being constant sources of encouragement and joy to our whole family.

OBJECT TALKS from Sports Kids Love

Published by Standard Publishing, Cincinnati, Ohio
www.standardpub.com

Copyright © 2004 Verna L. Kokmeyer
All rights reserved. #25594. Manufactured in Fredericksburg, VA, USA, January 2012.
No part of this book may be reproduced in any form, except for brief quotations in review, without the written permission of the publisher.

Cover design by Malwitz Design
Edited by Christine Spence

All Scripture quotations, unless otherwise indicated, are taken from the HOLY BIBLE, *NEW INTERNATIONAL VERSION*® NIV®. Copyright © 1973, 1978, 1984 by Biblica, Inc.™ Used by permission of Zondervan Publishing House. All rights reserved.

Scripture quotations marked *(NLT)* are taken from the Holy Bible, *New Living Translation,* copyright © 1996. Used by permission of Tyndale House Publishers, Inc., Wheaton, Illinois 60189. All rights reserved.

17 16 15 14 13 12   7 8 9 10 11 12 13 14 15
ISBN-13: 978-0-7847-1602-1
ISBN-10: 0-7847-1602-1

CONTENTS

BULL'S EYE

Theme: pleasing God

Sport: archery

Materials: target on which you can write, marker, smaller paper targets for each child, markers or colored pencils

Scripture: 2 Corinthians 5:9
"So our aim is to please him always" (NLT).

WARM-UP

Ready . . . aim . . . shoot. Archery is an old sport, but it's still a favorite of many. While some people hunt with a bow and arrow, others shoot arrows for fun or in competition. To get ready, they set a target several feet away. Then they take aim at the bull's eye, pull back the arrow on the string, and shoot.

If you hit the bull's eye you get ten points. (*Point to on the target.*) That's the best shot you can make. You get fewer points when you hit further from the center of the target. If your arrow hits the outside ring (*show*), you only get one point.

Many shots don't count. Hitting the ground in front of the target is worthless. Breaking the window of the house next door only makes you lose points with your neighbor. Even if your arrow hits a tree way, way across the road, your impressive long shot doesn't earn you any points. You don't even get any points for slipping and hitting yourself in the foot. The only way to get points is to take aim and hit the target—and especially the bull's eye.

As Christians, we also need to take aim. The Bible reminds us that our aim should be to please God. (*Read the Scripture.*) Too often we miss the mark. Sometimes we fail to appreciate what God or others have done for us. We may lose our patience with other kids and even call them names. Sometimes we hurt ourselves because friends no longer want to hang around with us. We don't get points for the times we fail to please God, or what we do only to impress others.

How can Christian boys and girls make God happy? (*Discuss.*) The Bible tells us that his most important commandment is to love God. (*Print "Love God" on bull's eye.*) Another important commandment is that we love others as ourselves. (*Write "Love Others" on the ring closest to the center.*) What other things make Jesus happy? (*Let children give ideas while you write them anywhere on the target. They might suggest sharing, praying, reading the Bible, obeying parents, helping others, and so on. Include practical ideas the children will understand.*)

SCOREBOARD

All of you do things to please God. We've already listed some. (*Point to the target.*) It is important to take aim, rather than just hope to please God. Let's each decide on something we can do to please God today. Who has an idea for something they would like to do? (*Helping parents, playing with younger siblings, being kind to the new kid at school, and so on.*)

POST GAME

(*Individual targets can be computer generated or made with paper and a protractor. Print the theme—Please God Always—leaving space for a personal goal. Make a copy for each child. You can copy in color, or encourage children to color their own targets. Give the children the targets and ask them to print or draw the ways they will please God on their targets.*) Hang your target where it will remind you to do what will please God.

PRAYER: Lord, our aim is to make you happy. May our actions always be pleasing to you. In Jesus' name, amen.

A TWEET GAME

Theme: God's Word

Sport: badminton

Materials: badminton birdie and racquet, feathers, note cards, marker, stapler

Scripture: Proverbs 19:2
"It is not good to have zeal without knowledge, nor to be hasty and miss the way."

WARM-UP

I can come out swinging. (*Demonstrate.*) Swish. Slam. Flick. Anyone can play badminton. Although the racket is kind of small, the birdie (*show*) falls a lot slower than a ball. That's because the birdie has feathers. Even if the birdie in your game doesn't have real bird feathers, it has plastic feathers, making it easier to hit than any ball.

I love the game of badminton. I can wind up and let the birdie have it. I can hit it straight up in the air. I can slash to the left and send it sailing. I can even slam it off to the right and try to hit the tree. Sometimes I get so excited that I miss the birdie entirely and it falls to the ground. Who cares! It is fun just playing with the racquet and the birdie.

One day a friend reminded me that all my enthusiasm would not necessarily make me win the game. I'm doing things that are wrong because I don't know how to play the game. There is a net I have to get the birdie over. I can't just whip it off to one side or the other. It goes out of bounds. I don't score if the birdie misses the racquet entirely. If I don't know about the game or obey the rules, I lose. Bummer. I can swing the racquet all I want, but all my excitement doesn't win the game.

Badminton is exciting, but Christians should be even more excited about serving Jesus. Along with our enthusiasm comes the importance of obeying God. His rules are for our own good. Rules keep us from doing things that would be harmful, and they protect us from danger. God gives us teachers, parents, and other adults to help keep us safe. We are obeying God when we follow their directions. Friends also need to remind each other about God's rules for our lives.

God gives us people to help us know more about him, and he also gave us an instruction book. Our Bible is God's Word, and it's full of his plans for our lives. As we learn about Jesus, his example shows us how we should behave. Knowing and obeying the rules keeps us from sinning.

God loves our excitement, but with our enthusiasm we must know how God wants us to live. (*Read the Scripture.*) Knowing the rules help us win a badminton game. We can also serve God best when we know the instructions in his Word.

SCOREBOARD

Why would God want us to be excited about being a Christian? (*Collect ideas—it shows our love is real and attracts other kids who do not know Jesus.*)

How can we help others celebrate knowing Jesus? (*Discuss possibilities including some special events to share Bible stories and sing favorite choruses.*)

What other instructions does God give if we are to serve him? (*Lead a discussion about not using bad words, telling others about him, sharing, helping, and so on.*)

POST GAME
Give each child a feather to remind them of the lesson of the badminton birdie. If you wish, you can staple the feather to a note card with today's verse: "It is not good to have zeal without knowledge" (Proverbs 19:2).

PRAYER: Lord, help us to study your Word so we can serve you with knowledge and excitement. In Jesus' name, amen.

STEALING BASES

Theme: opportunities

Sport: baseball

Materials: baseball base, gray construction paper, scissors, marker

Scripture: Colossians 4:2-6
 "Be wise in the way you act toward outsiders; make the most of every opportunity" (v. 5).

WARM-UP
I like the game of baseball, but there is one thing I don't understand. What's the big deal about stealing a base? (*Show the base.*) I can't even imagine why someone would want a base, much less steal it. Yet, I know that's a goal for all baseball players. Players tell me it's not an easy thing to do. Oh, I know a lot of fans are watching the field. Even the umpires might be around. You'd have to do it fast. How hard can it be? You just need to run out on the field, bend over to pick up the base, and go hide it under the bleachers. Nothing to it. What is so hard about stealing a base?

(*Allow time for kids to react.*) What? Stealing a base is not the same as taking a base that does not belong to you? (*No.*) You guys are right. I'm teasing you. Most of us know that stealing a base involves running to the next base while the other team is not looking. If you are on first, you might sneak to steal second. If you are on second, maybe you will be able to make it to third or even slide into home.

A baseball player has choices. When he hits the ball, he can run from one base to another unless tagged out by the other team. Once he gets on base, the player can make the use of every opportunity to steal bases. It's not easy. Do you know why it's hard to steal bases? (*Get input about how the other team wants to get you out.*) Players have to be determined. Often their teammates are close to the bases, so they can encourage runners.

As Christians, we are also called on to be wise and make the most of every opportunity, not to steal bases but to tell others about Jesus Christ. (*Read the Scripture.*) You have choices. Many children do not know that Jesus died to save us from our sins. You can invite other kids to church or Sunday school. If there are special Christian events, you can invite them to come with you. Friends can help each other invite and make visitors feel welcomed. It isn't always easy sharing Jesus Christ with others. Why is that sometimes hard? (*Discuss: We might be too shy. It can be scary to share with kids we don't know well.*) Like in a baseball game, where the other team tries to stop the runner, Satan doesn't want others to know about Jesus Christ. Christians must encourage one another.

A team is most likely to win when players take every opportunity to steal bases. That makes their fans very happy, but it is much more important to please God by taking every opportunity to tell others about him.

SCOREBOARD
In what ways can you tell others about Jesus? (*Share other ideas, such as listening to Christian radio shows for kids or wearing Christian t-shirts.*)

POST GAME
Give each child his own "home plate." Cut the squares out of gray colored paper. Write on each the words: "Take every opportunity to share Jesus." Encourage the kids to keep the squares in their pockets, reminding them to share Jesus.

PRAYER: Lord, help us to take every opportunity to share you with our friends who do not know you. Work in their hearts, so they will love you too. In Jesus' name, amen.

SLAM DUNK

Theme: teamwork

Sport: basketball

Materials: basketball, paper, marker, scissors

Scripture: Colossians 3:12-17

"Bear with each other and forgive . . . as the Lord forgave you. . . .
And over all these virtues put on love, which binds them all
together in perfect unity" (vv. 13, 14).

WARM-UP

You can scream at the top of your lungs, and no one will tell you to be quiet.
Cheerleaders do cartwheels. People holler encouragement with mouths full of
popcorn, and guys in striped shirts try to blow whistles louder than the roar
of the crowd. Basketball games are fun to attend. Five athletes on one team
try to get a ball through the hoop at one end of the gym, while five others in
different colored shirts try to get the ball through the hoop on the other side.

While you see a lot of good moves, there is one thing you never see. It's
against the rules to grab the ball and carry it while you run lickety split across
the whole gym. That kind of running is called traveling, and when it's done, the
other team gets the ball. A player must bounce the ball or pass it to a team-
mate. If someone makes a mistake or misses the hoop, others need to forgive
and keep playing hard. You can't win the game if you're busy fighting with your
teammates or the other team.

What you do see in a basketball game is a lot of bouncing and throwing the
ball to team members. Thump . . . thump, thump . . . thump, thump, thump . . .
thump—all the time the ball is moved from one side of the gym toward the
goal. If you watch, Curtis may throw the ball to Luke, who bounces it to Jacob,
who finally jumps as high as he can to throw it in the hoop to score points.
Players constantly bounce the ball on the floor. Friends who watch shout
encouragement. Basketball is all about teamwork.

Being a Christian takes teamwork too. Our goal is to serve Jesus and introduce others to him. That's not easy to do all by yourself, and God's Word tells us to work together. Just as players constantly bounce the ball on the floor to move it toward the goal, we must constantly stay in touch with God through frequent prayer and Bible reading. If anyone makes a mistake, like the basketball players, Christians must forgive. It's easier to talk to others about Jesus when we have good friends to help and encourage. We are all part of a team. *(Read the Scripture.)*

Basketball players are rewarded by winning. God rewards us too. He takes care of us when we follow his rules. Any boy or girl can be a winner on the basketball court and in the family of God.

SCOREBOARD

Why is forgiveness important if we are to be part of a team? *(We must forgive as God forgave us. To show love and work together, we must forgive.)*

What things can you do as a team that are harder to do all alone? *(Prayer support, encouragement, answering questions, and so on.)*

POST GAME

Accordion-fold a piece of paper. On the fold draw one half of a person with the arms reaching to the other side of the paper. Cut out the person in advance or instruct kids to do it at home. Write the Bible verse on the torso of the top figure. After cutting along the lines you have drawn, the student will unfold to find a "team" of cutouts with hands joined.

PRAYER: Dear Lord, we thank you for making us a team of Christian boys and girls. Help us to serve you together. In Jesus' name, amen.

GIVING A GIFT TO THE GIVER

Theme: talents

Sport: bobsledding

Materials: picture of a bobsled team, candy

Scripture: Romans 12:1-8
   "We have different gifts, according to the grace given us" (v. 6).

WARM-UP

You'd think it would take your breath away. The people in a bobsled reach speeds of 80-90 miles per hour. A four man team includes a driver and others called pushers. Usually team members are recruited from other sports, like track or football, where the guys are fast runners. Pushers put on shoes with little spikes to cut through the ice and keep them from slipping when they push the sled off to a fast start. They've all practiced hard, so they can jump onboard in a flash. The goal is to be the fastest sled.

The driver steers so the sled goes fast, even around the curves. He needs to watch carefully and react quickly as the bobsled races down the hill. He can't race a bobsled by himself. If anyone spends time looking at the scenery, the sled could lose some speed. Leaning the wrong way could cause disaster. After crossing the finish line the guy in the back of the sled engages a metal claw which drags in the ice to make the sled stop. The bobsled team needs every-one to do his job exactly right to win the race. Together they have an opportunity to win the race.

We are not on a bobsled, but Christians are each given a job. We often use many of our talents in the church. Some of us are good leaders, and others know how to teach so people learn easily. *(Read the Scripture.)* Grown-ups often learn from kids. Other Christians encourage. You may be able to make people feel good about themselves by showing appreciation. Encouragers also keep others from getting tired by helping. A few of you may have good singing voices or play an instrument. You can share your talents with others in your church.

Unfortunately, sometimes when we share talents, problems arise. Michaela may think she sings better than Caitlin, and may feel bad she isn't asked to sing as often. Anna may believe she is a better helper in the nursery than Cooper, and gets mad because he gets to work there more often. Lindsay may always get to make popcorn when the kids meet, while others are angry because they don't get more turns. Often we criticize others because we think we could have done better. This can slow down the process of bringing others to Jesus.

We may need to be reminded that there is more than enough work to go around and every job is important. Helping is no less important than leading. Encouragement is needed just as much as other things we see people do.

Like the bobsledders each have a job, God gives each of us work that needs to be done to the best of our ability. Like the bobsled team we must not get distracted. We must reach the goal of having God use us and our churches to serve him.

SCOREBOARD

What are some talents God has given you?

What are some things you can do to help at church by using your talents? (*Discuss: Help clean up the classroom, make friends with visitors, help out with younger classes, and so on.*)

POST GAME

A talent is something given to us by God to share with others. I have some candy I'm going to give you. Usually it is for you to eat. This time, I want you to share some of it with someone else as a reminder of today's lesson.

PRAYER: We thank you, God, for giving us each talents to be shared. May we use them to serve you. In Jesus' name, amen.

SPARE!

Theme: forgiveness

Sport: bowling

Materials: bowling ball, white cardboard, scissors, marker

Scripture: 1 John 1:9
"If we confess our sins, he is faithful and just and will forgive us our sins."

WARM-UP

I'm not very good at bowling. I have friends who are better. It doesn't take a lot of equipment. You put your fingers in the holes of a very heavy ball. (*Show.*) You put shoes on that slide a little—but hopefully not enough to allow you to fall flat on your face. Then you bowl. You take careful aim and roll the ball down the alley. Roll, not throw. Some people just set the ball down and let it roll slowly. Others throw as hard and fast as they can. The goal is to roll the ball down the alley and knock over as many pins as possible.

It is possible to swing the ball back and have it go in the direction of the friends you are playing with, instead of down towards the pins. There have been times my ball went a ways in the air before it dropped down on the alley. Don't do that. You will get a dirty look from the person who owns the place. The alley is narrow, and it isn't easy keeping the ball in the alley instead of the gutter. Sometimes I've slipped, and the ball went right into one of the gutters on either side of the alley. If you get a gutter ball, no pins fall over.

You may feel bad after the first time you roll the ball. You'll be sorry if you missed the alley or left many of the pins standing. There is one thing about bowling that few other sports have. Listen to this—it's exactly why I love bowling. Even if you miss the pins entirely, you get a second chance. You can take a better aim. You can walk more carefully. You can get a tighter hold of the ball or keep your friends from distracting you. You still may be able to get a spare—all of the pins down on your second chance. I like to be part of a sport where I get a second chance.

Just as you get a second chance in bowling, God gives each of us another chance in life. Sometimes you might feel very sorry for some mistake you've made or a bad thing you've done. It is not easy to do right always; it's even harder than rolling a ball down a narrow alley. Maybe you were nasty to a friend or talked back to your mom. It's possible you are sorry for taking something that didn't belong to you. You know what? Just like we get a second chance in bowling, if we are sorry and ask God to forgive, he always gives us another opportunity to serve him faithfully. *(Read the Scripture.)* That's exactly what I love about serving Jesus.

If I mess up on my second chance to score in bowling, I have to wait for the next turn to try to catch up. In bowling I get fewer points with my second chance. God, however, forgives when we confess our sins, and his forgiveness is complete.

SCOREBOARD

How do we ask for forgiveness? *(Prayer.)*

How often will God forgive us? *(Discuss: Because we belong to Jesus he will always forgive. He wants to know we are sorry and will try to do better.)*

POST GAME

Cut white cardboard handouts in the shape of bowling pins. Write on each "God Forgives."

PRAYER: Lord, thank you for forgiving when we make mistakes. In Jesus' name, amen.

SEND HIM

Theme: love

Sport: croquet

Materials: croquet mallet, construction paper circles, marker, and a ball

Scripture: John 15:12
   "My command is this: Love each other as I have loved you."

WARM-UP

Croquet is a great game. Take one sunny day and a nice grassy, flat yard. The mallet is handy, not just for hitting the ball but also for pounding in the stakes.

After you pound a stake in on each end, you can arrange the hoops where they are supposed to go. Everyone gets a different colored ball. The goal is to get your ball through the hoops and back to the first stake before anyone else does.

It's fun to hit your ball through the hoops, but that's not my favorite thing to do. If you see that someone is getting ahead of you, you can stop trying to get through the hoops for a turn, and "send" another player's ball as far away from the goal as possible. All you have to do is hit his ball with yours. When the two balls are close together, one might think you are being friendly. Nothing is farther from the truth. You are allowed to put your foot on your ball and hit it hard with your mallet. *(Demonstrate softly.)* When your ball bumps the other player's, his will go flying. Bump—there goes Madeline's ball into a mud puddle. Bang—Mason's ball goes under the swing set. Kerplunk—Sammy's ball goes way behind the sandbox. You can make it harder for others to win by sending them.

One way to win in croquet is to make things difficult for others, but that is not how God wants us to treat others in real life. Life is not a game where we are trying to beat others. Jesus tells us to love others as much as he loves us. *(Read the Scripture.)* Do you think he loves us a lot? *(Discuss: He loved us so much he died for us.)*

Most of us play sports or games with others. How should we act toward our opponents? Should we be angry when another player is winning? *(Discuss good sportsmanship.)* Suppose you wanted to be the best speller in your class, and someone else won by spelling an easy word while you got stuck with a hum-dinger? Would you still be able to be kind? *(Get input.)* We need to be happy for the winner.

Sometimes the one who is ahead of others in a game needs to be more sensitive. Some teasing may be fun, but we must guard against making others feel bad. There are always those who have more and those who have less than we do. Jesus wants us to be kind to all.

There are times in life when we'd all like to "send" someone far away from us. God's Word commands we love others as Christ loved us. If we imitate Jesus Christ, croquet may be the only chance we get to slam someone. I guess that's what makes it fun—even for Christian kids.

SCOREBOARD
Why do you suppose God loves us so much? *(Discuss: He created us, we are his children, Jesus died for our sins, and so on.)*

Why is it important for us to love others? (*Our obedience to God makes our world a better place.*)

How can we act more accepting toward others? (*Pray for selves and others*)

POST GAME
Make circles out of construction paper about the size of croquet balls. Write on each circle: "Love others."

PRAYER: God, it's not always easy, but help us love others as you love us. In Jesus' name, amen.

UPS AND DOWNS

Theme: difficulties

Sport: cross-country skiing

Materials: skis or picture, small water bottles, self-stick labels, marker

Scripture: John 16:33
> "I have told you these things, so that in me you may have peace. In this world you will have trouble. But take heart! I have overcome the world."

WARM-UP
Cross-country skiing in the woods on a winter day is a beautiful experience. Let me tell you, there are gorgeous trails with great scenery from beginning to end. Left . . . right . . . left . . . right, your skis slide smoothly on top of the snow. Sometimes you go by a frozen lake or between huge trees and snow-covered rocks. Then it comes. You find yourself standing on the top of a hill. Speeding down a slippery hillside is the best part. It can be hard to steer, but that only adds to the excitement. Your skis give you a smooth ride around curves, until after a long ride, you finally get to the bottom of the hill. It's wonderful, especially if you missed the tree.

As you continue down the trail, you hope the next ride down a hill comes soon. Oh, no. There is a problem ahead. It was a wonderful ride down, but now the trail goes up. Going up is no fun at all. You have to dig in with your poles as you step up the hill. About halfway up, your left foot loses grip on the icy trail. You almost lose your balance. Then your right foot slides off to the right, and you sit down to keep from sliding down the hill. The goal is to get to the end of the trail, but you wish you were already there. It's hard to remember what fun it was going down one hill, after you have suffered climbing up the next. By the time you get to the top of the hill, you are out of breath and exhausted.

You might love cross country skiing, but it sure does have its ups and downs. That's what life is often like. I love it when everything goes along perfectly. I'm sure you are happy when you do well at school and your mom cooks your favorite dinner. Unfortunately, there are also the days when your best friend is home from school sick or the dog ate your homework, and you can't wait for the end of the day. Then you discover dinner is liver or spinach.

That's when our verse becomes especially important. (Read the Scripture.) Like the skier digging in with his poles, you may try to do it on your own, but that's impossible. Jesus knows we will have trouble, but he reminds us that he has already overcome any problems we could have. He promises to be with us always—on the ski trail, at your school—everywhere. As Christians we have a goal even greater than the end of the trail. Christians look forward to being with Jesus in heaven.

SCOREBOARD

What kinds of difficult experiences do kids have? (List some problems.)

How can Jesus help us? (Match to some of the difficult experiences above: comfort, joy, help to do right, and so on.)

POST GAME

There is something that reminds me of God's constant care. A cool drink of water is always welcome. I have a drink of water in a bottle for each of you so you can remember our lesson about God's help for you.

(Pass out small water bottles. You may want to add your own "label" John 16:33 printed on it.)

PRAYER: God, thank you for being with us in fun times and difficult times. Our peace comes from always having you with us. In Jesus' name, amen.

SNOWPLOWING

Theme: temptation

Sport: downhill skiing

Materials: skis, cardboard, scissors, marker, construction paper, and brads (optional)

Scripture: 1 Corinthians 10:13
"No temptation has seized you except what is common to man. And God is faithful; he will not let you be tempted beyond what you can bear. But when you are tempted, he will also provide a way out so that you can stand up under it."

WARM-UP

The hardest part of downhill skiing is getting down a steep hill without wiping out. Nobody wants to break an arm or a leg and have to wear a cast until it heals. Even if you don't get hurt when you fall, it's hard to get up if your skis are still on and even harder to put them on if they are not. Skiing is not for sissies. More than anything else, it's important to know how to stop in the middle of the steepest hill.

A safe beginner needs to learn how to snowplow. Snowplowing involves moving your feet so the tips of your skis are close to each other and the other ends far apart. (*Demonstrate, or have a friend sitting in a chair show the kids.*) It's not easy. If your skis stay next to each other (*show*), you go straight down the hill. If the toes cross (*show*), you are sure to wipe out. Ski instructors help you learn to make this pie-shaped wedge with your skis. That is why you see them shouting "pizza, pizza, pizza" from behind people who are skiing too fast down the slope. When you do get in the snowplow position, with knees bent, the long edge of your skis push against the snow. Unless you learn to snowplow well, you will pick up speed and might find yourself flying to the bottom and on through the window of the place where you buy hot cocoa.

Snowplowing takes practice. Most people start on the bunny hill. When they are able to stop there, they get the confidence to take a chairlift up to a more difficult hill. Soon you learn that you are able to stop yourself on any hill, saving yourself a lot of pain.

Just as learning to snowplow avoids the pain of falling on the slopes, Christians need to learn how to avoid being tempted to do things that cause us other kinds of pain. If we're tempted to tell a little white lie, it becomes easier to tell a bigger lie. If we choose to steal something small, later it is easier to take something more valuable. Sin always results in pain.

We must learn to stop right from the start—while we are still young. It isn't easy. It takes practice. There will be times when we fail, but being successful in the little things will lead to success over difficult temptations. God gives us strength. (Read the Scripture.)

When learning to ski, snowplow against the snow. Every day we must fight against the temptation to do wrong.

SCOREBOARD

Why is it so easy to be tempted? (It seems to be the easy way out, or the result looks like fun. We may doubt we will be caught.)

Is it really possible to get away with being tempted and doing something wrong? (Discuss: God sees all.)

POST GAME

Give each child two cardboard "skis" about 1 x 5 inches. Write on one "God will not let you be tempted beyond what you can bear." Add a narrow piece of cardboard as a crosspiece between the two skis. Attach with brads so that the skis can turn to snowplow.

PRAYER: Lord, thank you for being faithful in helping us resist temptation. In Jesus' name, amen.

A LICENSE TO FISH

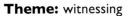

Theme: witnessing

Sport: fishing

Materials: fishing pole, goldfish crackers

Scripture: Mark 1:17
"'Come follow me,' Jesus said, 'and I will make you fishers of men.'"

WARM-UP

It takes some help to become a great fisherperson. It's more complicated than one might think. Let me demonstrate. I have this trusty fishing pole, and I've heard about casting. Watch this arm action. (*Demonstrate.*) I'll just swing the pole back (*do*) and then forward. There we go. How long will we have to wait for a fish? (*A long time without having what is needed for fishing.*) You're telling me, it's not likely I'll catch a fish like this. (*No?*) You're telling me I'll never catch a fish this way? Hmmmm. What am I doing wrong? (*Get suggestions.*)

Okay, so first of all I have to go somewhere near water. That makes sense. Oh, yes, I also need some strong line in my pole. Line goes on the reel. What else? (*Have children contribute ideas.*) I will need some bait. What does bait do? (*Attract the fish with something that looks good to him.*) It sounds like I should study what fish like—maybe offer them something they can't live without. A lot of fish are caught on live bait. I'll get some of that and a hook. If I do these things, the best fish will be mine, right? (*Right.*)

Come to think of it, there is another little problem. Does anyone have a clue as to what we do with a fish when we catch him? (*Clean him so it can be used.*)

Some of us are fishers of fish, but the Bible teaches us to be fishers of men. (*Read the Scripture.*) What does that mean? (*Tell others about Jesus so they become his.*) If we are going to be a fisher of kids, we need to make sure we spend some time near children who don't know Jesus. If we want to be with kids who don't know Jesus, would we spend all of our time in church? (*No, we will also want to witness at other places, including school.*) When we imitate Jesus, others will want to know him. To catch fish, I have to study what fish like.

Where do I learn how to bring people to Jesus? *(The Bible tells us that the Holy Spirit will work in children's hearts if we tell them about Jesus and show God's love for them.)* We already know that kids who know Jesus have what no one would want to live without.

What happens to our friends after they come to know Jesus? They will need our friendship to grow as Christians. We will want to invite them to church and Sunday school. Kids who accept Jesus will want to learn more about Jesus, and take up the sport of fishing themselves.

SCOREBOARD

Jesus said, "I will make you fishers of men." Why can't we just go ahead and try to catch people on our own? *(We need help to become a great fisher of people. People are brought to Jesus only through God's working in them. If we are close to him, God will lead us and work in the hearts of people who do not know him.)*

POST GAME

God will make us fishers of men. Remind children by giving each child some fish— goldfish crackers.

PRAYER: Lord, work through us so that our words and actions will help other people come to know you. In Jesus' name, amen.

TOUCHDOWN

Theme: victory

Sport: football

Materials: football, small jewelry or craft boxes

Scripture: I Corinthians 15:55-57
"But thanks be to God! He gives us the victory through our Lord Jesus Christ" (v. 57).

WARM-UP

Football is for tough guys. You know what I mean. The goal is for one team to get the football to one side of the field, while the other team tries to get it over to the goal line on the other side of the field. The guys who get the most touchdowns and extra points get the victory.

Between the goal posts, each team attacks the other in an effort to get the ball for their team. It gets rough out there. If you don't have the ball, you won't have much of a problem. The guy with the ball has a big problem. He must run, throw, or get slammed. Guys on the other team are always ready to tackle him. Others plow into him and drive him out of bounds. Scoring seems impossible. More often than not they all end up in a big pile somewhere on the field. I like to watch football action, but I'd never want to be on the bottom of the pile. Football players are big—very big. You or I would be like a little splat needing to be scraped off the turf. I couldn't play football with the big guys. With my size and all of the mistakes I'd make, we'd lose any game for sure.

Life is as difficult as a football game, and most of us make mistakes. Sometimes after a long day at school, we regret that we acted a certain way. If you were nasty to a friend, you might wish that you could take back something you said in anger. Have you ever had that happen to you? (Yes.) Most of us have. The Bible tells us that we all sin and were once headed for punishment. That's scary. Have you ever done something wrong and known for sure that you would be punished when your mom or dad came home? (Yes.) I won't even ask you what you did. Didn't you just dread the punishment? That's like having a whole team of big football players coming at you with nowhere to hide. Having parents or friends forgive you makes you feel much better.

At first, victory over sin may seem as hopeless as the idea of your winning a football game. You may want to serve God, but like the football player who carries the ball, the harder you try to live a life for Jesus, the more problems seem to come your way. God has the answer. God knew we would never be able to save ourselves, much less win a victory. The only way to have victory over sin was for God to send Jesus. It doesn't matter if we are large or small. Jesus not only took our punishment, but he also left an empty tomb when he rose, giving us the victory.

A football victory is cause for a one time celebration. God promises victory for us through Jesus Christ when he lives in us. (Read the Scripture.)

SCOREBOARD

Why is it so important that Jesus rose? (He must be alive to be our Savior.)

How does Jesus help you win out over sin? (Through his words in the Bible, through prayer, through parents and friends who give us good examples, and so on.)

POST GAME

Jesus died for us, but salvation came through his rising again, leaving the tomb empty. I'm giving each of you something to remind you of the empty tomb. (*Give each child a small empty jewelry or craft box. Write on the inside bottom: "God gives us the victory through our Lord Jesus Christ."*)

PRAYER: Dear Jesus, we celebrate your victory as our risen Lord. In Jesus' name, amen.

FORE!

Theme: obedience

Sport: golf

Materials: golf club, construction paper, straws, hole punch, scissors

Scripture: Proverbs 8:10
> "Choose my instruction instead of silver, knowledge rather than choice gold."

WARM-UP

Golfers can be a little crazy. Rain or shine they are out on the course chasing a small, white ball over hills and across the fields. Some of them follow on foot, but others ride around in a special little cart. They get in and out of the cart to hit the ball. If you are really a good player, you can get someone else to carry your clubs and even give you advice.

I'd be a real tiger on the course if I could play the game my way. For instance, when you want the ball to go a great distance, why hit it with a skinny club? (*Show.*) It would go farther if I could use a bat. Players of the game use a tee to get the ball off the ground for a good shot. Why not have a special tee made that is much taller so that I wouldn't have to bend so far? It's not my fault if my ball keeps heading for the water. Why should I be penalized? The thing that bugs me most is that the golfer with the fewest strokes always wins. That isn't fair. I walk farther, and use much more energy hitting the golf ball so often. I think the one with the most strokes should be the winner. Every golfer wants a hole in one. Why not get a hole in ten? Doesn't that sound good to all of you? (*No, it changes the game.*)

I guess maybe it wouldn't be so good. Anyway, I'm afraid I might have a problem finding anyone to play using my preferences. Why would playing golf like I want to be a problem? (*The game of golf has rules that must be followed.*) No great game is played without rules.

Most people can understand why games need rules, but they have more trouble understanding why our lives need rules. I don't like some of the rules I need to follow, and I'm sure you have some you don't like either. When I was young, there was a rule about my going to bed at a certain time. There were also rules about what time I had to be at school. I didn't like rules. I forgot that sleep was needed to be healthy, and that time at school was needed to learn important things, like how to read. Rules are valuable.

The most important rules are those God gives us. Our verse today reminds us to put God's rules first. (*Read the Scripture.*) That may seem like a bummer until we realize how impossible it is to live without rules. The Christian wins with God's rules.

SCOREBOARD

God's rules include the Ten Commandments. Why are God's rules more important than any other rules in our lives? (*They were given to us by God who made us and he knows what is best for us. Game rules are man made.*)

How do God's rules help us? (*Obeying God keeps us from sinning and keeps us doing what honors him.*)

POST GAME

Give each child a triangular flag like those which mark the holes on a golf course. To make flags, cut construction paper into triangles, hole punch two holes along one side and slide a straw through the holes. Print on each flag the words, "Choose my instructions."

PRAYER: God, help us to serve you by obeying your laws. In Jesus' name, amen.

TRIPLE BACK FLIP

Theme: God's power

Sport: gymnastics

Materials: picture of gymnasts, paper, markers

Scripture: Colossians 1:28, 29
"To this end I labor, struggling with all his energy, which so powerfully works in me" (v. 29).

WARM-UP

Have you seen gymnastics in person or on television? Most of us have. A gymnast goes in front of a huge crowd of people and starts a routine. It is unbelievable to see what a gymnast can do. The athlete jumps high and braces himself on a bar. Soon he catches other bars in his hands and, just when you think he might fall on the ground, the crowd gasps as he flips in the air from one bar to another. How can a person do such incredible feats?

No doubt the athletes take good care of their bodies and practice for the competition. I'd guess they choose the best food and never argue with their moms about taking vitamins. They exercise and learn from a coach for hours at a time. Where do they get the energy? The routines look impossible. It would be impossible for me.

When the routine is finished, the judging begins. Giant numbers appear on the board. If the routine was especially good, the athlete might get all 10s. That's the best you can get. Other times, the most fantastic routines—the ones that impress me the most—get lower scores. I wouldn't be a very good judge.

As a Christian, our work is to serve God. Sometimes it seems impossible. You are all still very young. Like the gymnast practices with a coach, we must prepare by staying close to God, with a heart willing to do what he asks. Sometimes we run around looking for good things to *do*, but God first wants us to *be*. We need to be in constant communication with him so we can know what he wants from us. God may want us to do something special for him, or give help to someone we haven't even met yet. If he wants us to tell a person about him, he will give us the opportunity and even help with the words to say.

One thing is sure. God gives each of us the strength and energy to do what he wants us to do for him. *(Read the Scripture.)* Whew! That's a relief, isn't it? *(Yes.)* He not only has a plan for our lives, but he also has power for me to get the work done.

Our final score won't be given by others. Someday God alone will judge us on how we used his energy to do the work he planned for us. What number would you want Jesus to give each of us for our score? Would a 5 be good enough? Would you settle for an 8? *(Discuss: As Christians we want God to be pleased with the work we have done.)* I pray that as our only judge, he will give us each a 10—the very best anyone could do.

SCOREBOARD

How do we know how God wants us to use his energy? *(Discuss: Some ideas include prayer and reading his Word. The advice of others who love him and us can sometimes help. We already know that energy should not be used to do wrong.)*

How can you use God's power and energy? What can you do for him?

POST GAME

Make an award sign for each of the children. Each should include a large number 10, and the message of our verse: "His energy works in me" (Colossians 1:29).

PRAYER: God, help us to do the tasks you choose for us, using the power and energy you give. In Jesus' name, amen.

GOAL TENDING

Theme: godliness

Sport: hockey

Materials: hockey puck, red construction paper hearts or red paper doilies, marker

Scripture: Proverbs 4:20-27
"Above all else, guard your heart, for it is the wellspring of life" (v. 23).

WARM-UP

I could never be a professional hockey player, but I think it would be fun to play hockey with my friends. I'd probably be the goalie. I don't ice skate too well, and I don't like the idea of being knocked over on the ice. But I would be pretty good at keeping the puck (show) out of the goal. Oh, I know it wouldn't be easy. You can't be caught sleeping. I'd be ready to protect the left side (move to left), and no one would be able to attack me from the right (jump to the right). I've watched hockey on television and I'd follow the example of the best players. They do almost anything to keep the other team from getting close and scoring. Of course I'd follow all the rules, but if all else failed, I'd spread out in front of the goal so nothing would get in. (Demonstrate by stretching arms above head and lean to the side.) Do you think that would work? (Maybe, but it's not as easy as one might think and might be dangerous.) The other team is going to try really hard to score, but I shouldn't have to worry about getting hurt, because I'd wear all the same equipment the big guys wear. I wouldn't let anyone score against us and my team would win for sure.

A hockey goalie protects the goal any way he can. That's exactly how God would have us protect our hearts. Jesus wants us to keep our heart pure by following all the rules God gives us in the Bible. All of us need to keep our eyes wide open and look both ways to keep out thoughts and actions that don't honor God. Jesus is our example. He always honored his Father, especially with his love for others. Remember how he was always kind and loved others? That sounds easy enough, doesn't it? (It's not always easy, especially if it involves younger brothers and sisters.) Satan is trying hard to get in and make us do wrong. We can win only if we keep evil and danger away. It's dangerous to let our guard down. We have to rely on God's protection.

All of us can get very excited about keeping the puck out of the goal at a hockey game, but we can be less concerned with keeping all of the dirty things out of our minds and hearts. The goalie will do anything to keep the puck from the goal. Christians must be just as determined to guard their hearts and lives from evil. With God's help, we can be strong winners with pure hearts. (Read the Scripture.)

SCOREBOARD

Jesus had a pure heart. How was that shown in his life? (Jesus could not be tempted to do wrong, he healed people, loved others—especially children, and so on.)

How do we know if our hearts are pure? (Our actions usually show what our hearts are like. A pure heart results in sharing, clean language, honesty, being kind even when someone is not nice to you, being helpful even to people we don't know, and so on.)

POST GAME

Cut hearts out of red construction paper, or purchase red, lace doilies. Print on each "Guard your heart."

PRAYER: Lord, help us to do everything we can to keep our hearts and lives clean and pure. In Jesus' name, amen.

BE LIFTED UP

Theme: humility

Sport: ice skating

Materials: ice skates, helium balloons, marker

Scripture: I Peter 5:6, 7
> "Humble yourselves ... that he may lift you up in due time. Cast all your anxiety on him because he cares for you."

WARM-UP

When you watch professionals skating, it looks easy. The skaters spin around and glide across the ice, right in time to the music. A pair of skaters skate together perfectly. They usually do many tricks and spins, exactly at the same time. They skate fast all around the rink. Then, when you least expect it, the guy lifts the girl high above his head. The man is always bigger and stronger. I've never seen a girl lift the guy off the ice. Have you? (*No.*) The girl has to be willing to let the man do all the work. She has to be humble and let him take credit for the hard work. At the same time, when lifted up, the girl doesn't have to skate at all. She just rides high above the ice.

Sometimes the girl's feet are held while the rest of her swings low and close to the ice. People who are watching often clap and cheer. They are amazed that her head doesn't hit the ice. While she must be an excellent skater, at that point the man is the one holding on to her and keeping her from falling. He has to be very strong. You'd think he would wipe out or just get tired and lose his grip. The girl always smiles, knowing he will keep her safe. He smiles too, as if nothing is too hard for him.

There are times in life when, like an ice skater, we need someone strong to lift us up. You kids are pretty big to be carried by a mom or a dad, but all of us have Jesus to lift us up. Only Jesus could lift us—that certainly couldn't be done the other way around. He wants us to be humble in asking for his help. If we ask for his help, it is always there, just at the right time. (Read the Scripture.)

It's important that we stay close to Him. God often lifts us up at unexpected times and in surprising ways. Sometimes we can only praise him when he surprises us with a special blessing.

Spectators applaud great ice skaters. Your friends may come to trust in Jesus because they see how he helps you. When you trust in Jesus, you never have to worry about God getting tired or dropping you. He is strong and you can depend on him to keep you safe. Unlike the ice skater, nothing is really too hard for Jesus.

SCOREBOARD
If we know Jesus can help us, why don't we ask for his help more often? (Discuss: We might be too proud or forget that God is there for us. We might think he doesn't care about the little things in our lives.)

(If appropriate to the occasion, you might ask for prayer requests from the children. You could lead in prayer or have the children participate in sentence prayers.)

POST GAME
Give each child a helium balloon. Write on the balloons: Jesus Lifts Me Up. If this message is shared during a worship service, you could promise to hand out before the children go home.

PRAYER: Thank you, Lord, for being strong and willing to lift us up. We are glad that nothing in our lives is too hard for you to take care of. In Jesus' name, amen.

HIGH GOAL

Theme: heaven

Sport: mountain/rock climbing

Materials: picture of mountain climber, pretzel sticks, resealable bags, self-stick labels (optional)

Scripture: Isaiah 33:15, 16
"He who walks righteously and speaks what is right . . . will dwell on the heights."

WARM-UP

Mountain climbing must be very hard. It would also be scary. (*Show a picture of someone climbing.*) Imagine climbing up the side of a cliff, far above the ground. Don't look down. One little slip and you would fall far below. One wrong step and you wouldn't survive. If you were very high, the air would be thin and you'd be short of breath.

A lot of equipment is designed to help. I've heard about sticky shoes and hooks you can plant in little crevices. A harness might save you if you use a rope to climb with others. Even so, it's dangerous.

While some mountain climbers say they climb mountains just because they are there, I think there would be a lot fewer mountain climbers if it weren't for the reward at the top. From the top of the mountain you can see far and wide. Even if the cold air blows against you, it must be like standing on top of the world. What an accomplishment! What a thrill! I wish I could skip the climbing part and just show up for the view at the top.

Sometimes life is like an uphill climb. Does it seem to you that some days are as hard as climbing a high mountain? Usually it starts when I can't find my shoes in the morning. Maybe your problem is missing the bus or friends who bug you. Then you get pages of homework when you had plans to play with the neighbor kids. Events that happen are difficult enough, but then as Christians we must react to all the things that happen in a way that is pleasing to God. It wouldn't be good to throw a shoe at the person who put my shoes where

I couldn't find them. It's not Christ-like to clobber the brother or sister who bugs you. You already know that it's right to do your homework before you play.

Just like reaching the top of the mountain after a long hard climb, God's Word promises us a reward for serving him. There is no way we can skip serving God and still earn the reward. Living for Jesus involves studying his Word so we know exactly what we are to say and do. He walks beside us. *(Read the Scripture.)*

The mountain climber's goal is to be on top of the mountain for the thrill of the accomplishment and to enjoy being there for a short time. Our goal is spending eternity in heaven with Jesus. Now that's a thrill!

SCOREBOARD

People notice when someone climbs a high mountain. What kinds of things could we do in our walk with Jesus that would show others our love for God? *(Discuss and encourage children to take actions that witness to others. This might include honesty, language that honors God, following Jesus' example, looking for ways to help others, and so on.)*

POST GAME

Most of us will never climb high mountains, but I pray that all of us will always walk with Jesus. I brought along some walking sticks to share with you. *(Share with the children "walking sticks" which are actually pretzel sticks. If you wish you can put a few in baggies and attach labels with Isaiah 33:15, 16 printed on them.)*

PRAYER: God, we praise you for the reward that is ours when we walk close to you. May our lives show our love for Jesus. In Jesus' name, amen.

ROLLING

Theme: guidance

Sport: rollerblading

Materials: inline skates, copies of a map or part of a map, marker

Scripture: Isaiah 48:17-19
> "I am the Lord your God, who teaches you what is best for you,
> who directs you in the way you should go" (v. 17).

WARM-UP

I'd be an excellent inline skater (*Show skates*), if only I could go at my own pace. If I go too fast, I lose my balance. On the other hand, if I go too slow, it takes a long time to get anywhere. Also, any little stone or leaf in the road makes me stop short. One speed—not to slow and not too fast—usually keeps me from ending up in the bushes.

These problems are bad enough, but without a doubt my biggest problem is that I can't turn. It kind of spoils the fun to think that while you can skate away from home, you might not be able to skate back home. I've watched skaters put the same foot in front of the other several times until they are going the other way. (*Show with skates.*) Have you tried that? Be careful. Any time one of my feet goes in front of the other, I trip myself. Although I don't recommend it, that is one way to stop. You might get hurt, but for someone who can't turn, it also gives you a chance to aim your feet in the other direction when you get up. Unless I fall, I'd much rather just keep going straight ahead.

It's not a huge problem for an inline skater to go his own way at his own speed, at least for a while, but Christians can miss God's best for them when they are determined to do their own thing. God may want us to turn away from something we are doing that does not honor Jesus. He may want us to take the right turn instead of making a choice that keeps us from his best for us. (*Read the Scripture.*)

Sometimes God gives people a dream of serving him in special ways or in certain jobs, but instead of following their dream, they feel more comfortable going in the same direction and doing the same things they have always done. It is good to be reminded that God knows what's best for us, and what he puts in our heart is often his best for us.

There will be bumps along the way, even when we follow God's direction. Sickness and accidents happen to Christians too. Like skates hitting stones or leaves, things won't always go our way. You may want to watch TV, but Jesus wants you to obey your dad who tells you to clean your room. You may want another cookie, while mom wants you to wait until after dinner. We can trust that God's direction brings what is best for us.

SCOREBOARD

Why is it so important for the Christian to go where God guides? *(Discuss: God knows what is best and will make us the happiest.)*

It would seem that if we are trying to follow Jesus, we should have no problems in our lives. Why do Christians have problems? *(Difficulties make us grow. We learn from problems and they draw us closer to Jesus, and so on.)*

POST GAME

Make a copy of a part of a map. Write on the copy: "God directs you in the way you should go" Isaiah 48:17. Make copies and give one to each child.

PRAYER: Dear Lord, we so often want to go our own way and do our own thing. Teach us to follow your direction. In Jesus' name, amen.

ROW, ROW, ROW YOURSELF

Theme: spiritual growth

Sport: rowing

Materials: oars, small plants or seed packets

Scripture: 2 Peter 3:14-18
"But grow in the grace and knowledge of our Lord and Savior Jesus Christ" (v. 18).

WARM-UP

How many of you have been out on a lake in a rowboat? There are sports that involve racing, but that's not necessary to have fun. You might stop to look for fish swimming in the water below, or put the oars down and have your lunch on the water where it is very peaceful. Usually you can hear birds singing and even hear other animals on the shore. It's wonderful to do nothing but sit in the boat.

Our Scripture today isn't about sitting quietly in a boat. If we compare how we should live to rowing, we are to move ahead, learning all we can. To move ahead, we have to row. Have you tried rowing the boat all by yourself? Rowing can be hard work, especially for children. Fortunately, the more time you spend rowing, the stronger you get. Using both arms is important. One time I decided that to keep both arms from getting tired, I'd just row with one arm. (*Demonstrate.*) Do you know what happens when you row with one oar? (*Go in circles.*) If we use only one oar on one side of the boat, we will go in circles. We'll never see or learn anything new while our boat goes round and round in the same area.

The Bible tells us we must keep learning more about Jesus Christ and his love for us. (*Read the Scripture.*) To do that we can't just keep singing the same songs or only going over the Bible Stories we already know. That would be like going in circles in a rowboat. How can we learn more about Jesus? (*Discuss: Bible study, prayer, Sunday school, and so on.*) Having others read to us is a great way to get to know him, but as you get older, it is time to begin reading and learning from the Bible on your own. There are even some versions of the Bible especially for children to read. It may seem easier to have others read to us, but as we work at it, we will become stronger and can learn on our own.

It's possible to just relax and not worry about learning more about Jesus. God does not want us to live that way. Rowing takes effort and energy. We must make the same effort to learn about Jesus and get to know him better. Every one of us —including all the adults—will get stronger as we study God's Word. That's what God expects.

SCOREBOARD

What is it that might make it difficult for you to learn more about Jesus? (*Talk about setting aside a time for reading and prayer. Encourage even young children to begin a regular quiet time. Share a personal testimony as to how God worked in you because of your devotions.*)

Why is it important that as we grow, we learn to read the Bible and pray on our own? *(Discuss the importance of a personal relationship with Jesus and how as we get older it is important not always to need help—to be able to do it on our own.)*

POST GAME
Give each child a small plant or a seed packet to remind them of the growth God desires in our spiritual lives.

PRAYER: Lord, help us to grow in how much we know about Jesus Christ. Teach us to study your Word so we can serve you better. In Jesus' name, amen.

10 K

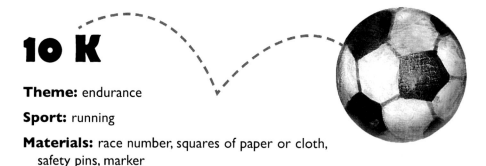

Theme: endurance

Sport: running

Materials: race number, squares of paper or cloth, safety pins, marker

Scripture: Colossians 1:9-14
> "Being strengthened with all power according to his glorious might so that you may have great endurance and patience, and joyfully giving thanks to the Father, who has qualified you to share in the inheritance of the saints in the kingdom of light" (vv. 11, 12).

WARM-UP
How many of you can run really fast? *(Have kids raise hands.)* Kids love to run. You may run to the store to get some candy. You might run to a friend's house to play. You might even run to school—or more likely—home from school. Most like to run fast for a short time, but do any of you like running for miles? *(Not many.)* It takes endurance to run for a long time. Most of us quickly get out of breath or our legs start aching.

Some people like to run so much that they practice every day. At first they go only a short distance, but each day they run farther. Two friends can encourage each other if they are both runners. If runners have drinking water along, they can quench their thirst without stopping. Some people compete in marathons by running twenty-six miles. There are rewards for those who complete the marathon in the least amount of time. There's a great celebration at the finish line, where winners are given trophies or medals. For other athletes, just being able to finish the long run is a reward itself.

There may be times when we are not winners in the race of life. We often fail to honor our Lord. We may make a wrong choice that leads us away from how we should live for him. It can be discouraging when we love Jesus but still do things that we know are wrong. Like the runners in races, we may not win all of the time. Yet, just knowing Jesus as Lord and Savior is a reward in itself.

If I survived a marathon, I would be ready for a nap. Running a race wouldn't be much fun—unless I was very well prepared. Endurance may take some time and effort to develop. Becoming a Christian who honors God all of the time seldom just happens. How do you suppose we get prepared to serve God? (*We prepare by being close to Jesus through prayer and Bible study.*) God gives us stamina to serve him. The better we know Jesus, the stronger we grow. God promises to give us patience when we get angry and joy when we might otherwise be sad. Christians often have friends to support them with prayer and encouraging words. Like the runner needs water along the way, Jesus gives thirsty Christians living water. When we get to the end of our lives, heaven is our reward. That's reason to celebrate. (*Read the Scripture.*)

SCOREBOARD

How do runners know when the race is over? (*The finish line is marked. A timer may even show how long it took you to finish.*)

When does the Christian stop serving and praising God? (*Serving God is a lifetime commitment. If we love Jesus, we will always want to grow in knowing about God and sharing him with others.*)

POST GAME

When you run a race you get a numbered square to safety pin to the front of your shirt. I have one for each of you. (*Make each child a similar square. In this case put "#2" in big letters. Under that print, "Jesus is First."*)

PRAYER: God, give us the endurance to serve you all of our lives. In Jesus' name, amen.

WHEN THE WIND BLOWS

Theme: success

Sport: sailing

Materials: sail or picture of sailboat, colored or printed squares of paper

Scripture: John 15:1-8

"I am the vine; you are the branches. If a man remains in me and I in him, he will bear much fruit; apart from me you can do nothing" (v. 5).

WARM-UP

There are some things you feel, even when you can't see anything. A good example is the wind. How many of you have felt the wind when it is blowing very hard? (*Pause for response.*) Wind messes up our hair and sometimes even takes papers out of our hands and blows them across the street. We have never seen the wind, but we sure can see what it does, can't we?

There are times when we need the wind. That's especially true when we want to go sailing. Have any of you ever been sailing? (*Show sail or picture.*) It's fun to sail, but you have to be careful. As soon as you start putting your sail up, the wind catches it and makes your boat move. On a small boat, you have to sit down right away or you might fall off. When the wind is very strong, your boat goes fast and it can tip over with you in it. If you want to sail, it doesn't hurt to know how to swim in case you fall in.

There may be other times when you are on a sailboat and the wind dies down completely. What happens to your boat then? (*Nothing. It stands still.*) Without wind you don't move in a sailboat. You may know that your family is cooking hamburgers on the grill, but unless the wind comes up, you won't be able to get there. (*Shake head sadly.*)

Wait a minute. (*Pause.*) I have an idea. Suppose you blow in the sail. Do you think that would make you move? (*No—pause.*) I've got it! Suppose you were with a friend and you both blew at the sail as hard as you could. Would that get the boat moving? (*No—not strong enough.*)

Just as the sailboat won't budge without wind, there is not much we can do without Jesus Christ. *(Read the Scripture.)* We can't see Jesus, but we can see what he does in people's lives. What changes come when we have Jesus working inside us? (*Discuss: We experience love, unselfishness, joy, helpfulness, and so on.*) We can especially see God's power when it comes to people accepting Jesus as Savior. We might try everything to talk a friend into becoming a Christian. We could even have another friend help us, but that's not something any of us have the power to do. God has given us an important part. We can tell our friends about Jesus and what he has done for us, but it is the Holy Spirit who works in their hearts. If they move to accept Jesus as Savior, it is only because God allowed us to be used.

Sailboats do nothing without the wind. Christians need Jesus to help them bring others to him.

SCOREBOARD

In addition to working in people's hearts so that they come to know him, what other things does God do for us? (*Discuss how God gives everything we have.*)

POST GAME

Make small accordion folded fans out of colored paper. Give each child a fan to remind them that just like they feel the unseen breeze, we do not see God but know his power in our lives.

PRAYER: God, we can do nothing without you, and we praise you for your power in our lives. In Jesus' name, amen.

SERVING WITH A WHOLE HEART

Theme: service

Sport: skateboarding

Materials: skateboard or picture, small date books or calendars, pens or pencils

Scripture: Ephesians 6:7
"Serve wholeheartedly, as if you were serving the Lord, not men, because you know that the Lord will reward everyone for whatever good he does."

WARM-UP

I would guess that once upon a time, skateboarding started when someone attached an old board to the wheels removed from a pair of roller skates. Imagine what riding on that board must have been like. When the first person carried the homemade board to the top of a hill, no doubt his only goal was to somehow stay on and avoid hitting anyone on the way down. More than a few trips down the hill would have qualified as a world's funniest home video, don't you think?

Now we can watch skateboarders perform impossible looking tricks. They soar through the air, and you'd think the specially designed boards were glued to their feet. I can't believe how high they fly above a half pipe. (*Discuss the tricks kids have seen.*) What once was an attempt to get down the hill in one piece, now involves spectacular tricks and different kinds of skateboarding. Some of the more famous guys even have tricks named after them—including those involving 360 and even 540 degree turns. Some skateboarders still do street skating, but others spend hours learning and practicing new skills. It must take lots of courage and determination. Skaters wholeheartedly commit to doing their very best. Then they entertain others with their tricks and even win awards for their abilities.

Just as skateboarders have wholehearted commitment, God's Word tells us to serve him wholeheartedly. (*Read the Scripture.*) Watching skateboarders gives the words "serve wholeheartedly" new meaning. When we first started to serve God, we no doubt improvised a bit. We didn't know many of the verses from Scripture, and we weren't sure how to reach our goal of sharing Jesus with others. It was an exciting time, but we probably made mistakes as we tried to witness to others.

As time goes on, it is possible to keep serving God in the same way we served from the start. Unless we commit to hours in the study of God's Word, we won't learn about new ways to serve him. If we forget to spend time in prayer, we won't get to know him better. Serving better takes courage and determination.

Christians must also serve others wholeheartedly. Someone in your church may be famous for making and sharing cinnamon rolls. Another person may be well known for visiting the sick. They are not only serving others, but also serving God.

People get awards for their skateboarding. The Bible promises Christians even better rewards for wholehearted service.

SCOREBOARD

We can all do better at serving God through helping others. What are some of the ways we can serve? (*Discuss while making a list of some creative things kids could do for others. Try to get the children beyond reading the Bible and praying to putting what they have learned into action.*)

What rewards does God give for serving him? (*Discuss: He gives heaven, the joy of sharing, Christian friends, people who help us, answered prayers, and so on.*)

POST GAME

Give each child a small date book or a copy of the month's calendar. Have them schedule some of the ideas you all have shared. If children are younger, have them ask mom or dad to help.

PRAYER: God, may we learn how to work for you, as we practice serving every day. In Jesus' name, amen.

DRIBBLE

Theme: protection

Sport: soccer

Materials: knee pads, cough drops or peppermints

Scripture: Proverbs 30:5
"Every word of God is flawless; he is a shield to those who take refuge in him."

WARM-UP

Does anyone know what sport you play with a ball and use any part of your body except your arms and hands? (*Soccer.*) You got it—soccer. If you play or watch soccer, you know that there are two different teams, and the teams always have different colored shirts so you know right away who is who. One team tries to get the soccer ball to the goal on one side of the field, while the other team wants the ball to go through the goal posts on the other side. To win, you have to follow the rules.

Usually players kick the ball, and a long kick by a member of one team makes half of the parents on the sidelines cheer. More often the ball is dribbled across the field with short pushes and kicks that often go from one player to another. You know how it goes. Mason kicks the ball over to his goal, but Jacob kicks it right back at him. Madeline dribbles the ball around the outside, but Anna stops it and kicks the ball the other way. When all the players are really good, it's hard for either team to score.

One thing is not hard. With twenty-two kids determined to get the ball in the goal and forty-four feet on the field, it is not hard to get kicked in the shin or hit by a ball. That must really hurt, don't you think? (*No—you're protected.*) It would really hurt if you didn't put on shin guards. If the pads were heavier, you would not be able to run fast with them on. Thinner pads would not protect nearly as well. With the plastic and padding, you have perfect protection that you can pretty much count on to keep you from getting black and blue legs.

Just as shin guards protect our legs when playing soccer, God and his Word provide a shield of protection for those who love him. (*Read the Scripture.*) We can depend on everything in his Word to be true, and following God's Word keeps us safely close to God. Like soccer shin pads, the Bible is perfect just the way it is. Some people want to change the Bible. They think it would be better if it didn't include some verses they don't like or maybe don't want to obey. There are also those who want to make an improvement by adding to God's Word. For the Bible to be useful protection, it can not be changed anymore than we can change the soccer rules to make our team win. Scripture lets us know that "every word of God is flawless." *Flawless* means perfect and that's as good as it gets.

God's flawless Word protects boys, girls, and adults who love Him, just as shin guards protect kids who like to play soccer. Imagine the protection kids have who love to serve Jesus *and* love to play soccer.

SCOREBOARD

What ways does God protect us? (*God gives us adults who love us to protect us. He gives doctors and policemen. He also gives us his Word, with rules designed to keep us safe, and so on.*)

POST GAME

To remind the children that the Lord is their protection, share something else that can help them—a cough drop or pink peppermint.

PRAYER: We celebrate your protection, Lord. Thank you for giving us your flawless Word to keep us safe. In Jesus' name, amen.

WATER LOGGED

Theme: service

Sport: swimming

Materials: picture of swimmers, cards on which you have printed Hebrews 12:2

Scripture: Hebrews 12:2
"Let us fix our eyes on Jesus, the author and perfecter of our faith, who for the joy set before him endured the cross, scorning its shame, and sat down at the right hand of the throne of God."

WARM-UP

How many of you know how to swim? (*Get input.*) Do any of you know how to do some different strokes? Are any of you able to do a side stroke? Do some of you know a back stroke? Usually, if you are really good at the strokes necessary to swim well, you can be a great swimmer.

Most great swimmers know how to race. They've practiced and when the competition comes, you can feel the tension at the starting point as swimmers line up on the side of the pool. Most competitions start with a fast dive in the pool. Instantly the swimmers move across the pool with strong strokes. They are careful to stay in their own lanes, which they can see painted on the bottom of the pool. They move so fast, you can hardly see them breathe. No energy is wasted on their perfected strokes. They've practiced turning, and if it is a longer race, the turn is fast and smooth.

Have you ever seen a swimmer stop and look around to make sure they are ahead? (*No.*) Do any swimmers stop in the middle of a race to shine their foggy goggles on their bathing suits? (*Of course not.*) Have you ever seen a swimmer stop and wave to his friends or family? How many good swimmers race using a dog paddle? The winner's goal is to swim the necessary laps in the shortest amount of time. Great swimmers focus on the goal, and swim with all their strength.

As Christians, who want to do their best at serving Jesus, we need to remember our goal. Swimmers don't get sidetracked. They have no time to goof off. If our goal is to love and serve God and tell others about him, we must do that with all of our strength. (*Read the Scripture.*)

There may be other things in our lives which make it hard to reach our goal. Can you think of some things which keep us from using our time to serve Jesus? (*Television, computer games, playing with our friends, and so on.*) While these may not be bad for us, they are a problem if they take our focus from what we must do for God. Anything done in excess can take time away from doing things that honor God.

Just as we all swim in different ways, we all serve God in different ways. The important thing is to stay focused and not get sidetracked from the goals God has for us.

SCOREBOARD

Why is it important for a Christian to be focused on their goal? (*If we are not focused, we go from one thing to another and God's purpose for our lives is forgotten.*)

A swimmer needs to keep swimming to stay afloat. What happens to us when we are content to do nothing? *(Like a swimmer sinks, we will miss opportunities to serve God.)*

POST GAME

When we fix our eyes on Jesus, we will do everything necessary to help others come to know Him. *(Give each child a card with the verse printed on it. Encourage them to keep it in a pocket, so they will not forget the goal.)*

PRAYER: Lord, may we always focus on serving you with our whole hearts. In Jesus' name, amen.

LOVE MEANS ALWAYS

Theme: love

Sport: tennis

Materials: tennis racket, white paper, construction paper, scissors, tape or stapler, markers or colored pencils

Scripture: 1 Corinthians 13
Love . . . "is never glad about injustice but rejoices whenever the truth wins out. Love never gives up, never loses faith, is always hopeful, and endures through every circumstance" (vv. 6, 7, NLT).

WARM-UP

Tennis would be easier if you didn't have to hit the small ball with a racket. If your swing misses the ball, it seems like there is no net in your racquet at all. *(Demonstrate swing.)* When you do hit the ball, often it goes straight up in the air or across the ground to hit the lady in the next court. Even when the ball goes the right way, if it's too low it bounces off the net. To win, you must hit a tennis ball to your opponent, way over on the other side of the net. You get points if the ball is not returned correctly. Every time you serve the ball, you play until somebody goofs. Here's where it gets interesting. Whenever you have no points, your score is called "love." Imagine that! If you start by serving the ball and your friend gets the point, the score would be "love - 15." As long as you keep losing the point, your score is always "love."

Let me tell you, it's not easy to have zero points while your friend is leading the game. I might start to get frustrated because I want to win the game. It takes a lot to keep smiling while your friend makes points and you only have "love." Some of us might wish that whoever we are playing would miss the ball or at least trip on the way out of the court. Tennis is not the easiest sport in which to have love.

Sometimes you have love in tennis, but Christians are to have love always—regardless of the tennis score. Few things are "always." Is anyone here always happy? (No.) Do any of you always want pizza for every single meal? (No.) Like in tennis, Christian love means putting others first. Having love is not always easy, but it is God's rule for our lives. God tells us that we must always look for the truth in each other and must defend others while always expecting the best of them. (Read the Scripture.) Our friends may not always do everything right, but loving means we must help each other grow to be better imitators of Jesus as we serve him together.

Once a tennis game is over, the love score is soon forgotten. When Christians have the kind of love that is always there, the encouragement we get from each other helps everyone serve God.

SCOREBOARD
Why is it sometimes hard to love others? (Discuss: Even as Christians we hurt each other. All of us are sinful.)

How can we show love and support for other Christians? (Pray for them. Encourage children to give other practical suggestions for showing love and support for others.)

POST GAME
Today I'm going to give you a special opportunity to show your love. I've put a frame around a place for you to draw a picture to encourage. You might want to include a verse from the Bible. Give it to someone special. (Cut out the center of a piece of construction paper and attach the "frame" on top of a sheet of white paper.)

PRAYER: Lord, help us to always love by putting others first. In Jesus' name, amen.

HIT IT!

Theme: service

Sport: water skiing

Materials: water skis and tow rope, 6-inch pieces of rope, tags to attach to rope pieces

Scripture: Joshua 24:14, 15
"But as for me and my household, we will serve the Lord" (v. 15).

WARM-UP

To be able to water ski, you must first be able to get up. First time skiers tend to drag while sitting in the water, but eventually you need to stand. While you are sitting in the water, waves threaten to knock you over. You need to face forward with your feet both aimed straight ahead. (*You or a helper can demonstrate with skis on your feet.*) Let's see. What else do we need? (*Pause.*) Can we ski without a boat? (*No.*) Of course, if you don't have a boat and a tow rope, you can forget it. They are necessities. I couldn't bring the boat, but I have a tow rope. (*Hold the handle or give to helper.*)

A new skier may find it hard to decide how far your feet should be apart. (*Demonstrate.*) If you are afraid they will hit each other, you might put them too far out to the sides. When one foot goes north and the other goes south, it's all over. Quick as a wink you will be pulled over the top and flat on your face. You need to let go of the rope, or the speed of your underwater swimming will match the speed of the boat. On the other hand, if you decide to put your feet too close together, you might tip over to one side or the other and never get up on your feet. Most of the problems come when a beginner is not sure what to do with his feet and tries everything. Have any of you ever seen that happen? (*Get input.*) The beginning skier needs help.

Like skiers need to decide how best to ski, people must decide how best to live. If you follow Jesus, there is a decision to make. You can't watch your language in church and Sunday school, while you use bad words the rest of the week. An imitator of Jesus Christ does not act loving sometimes, and be nasty the rest of the time. The Christian must stand up for what he believes all of the time. Like a new skier hit by waves, learning to stand up is not always easy. Too often we hang on to old ways and, like the skier who hangs on to the rope, we can get dragged under to where we no longer honor God.

The skier can't ski without a boat and rope to pull him up. The Christian also needs help. Who can we get help from? (*God.*) Can we serve God without our Lord's help? (*No way.*) He works in our hearts, helping us to take a stand for Jesus and serve him all of the time.

It's a great feeling to get pulled up to a standing position on skis. It's much more exciting when, with his help, we stand up for Jesus Christ. (*Read the Scripture.*)

SCOREBOARD
If we decide to serve God, how can we get help from him? (*Discuss: We get help through reading the Bible to get our instructions, and asking for help in prayer.*)

POST GAME
Give each child a six-inch piece of rope to remind them that God is able to help us as we stand up to serve Him. You can attach a tag to each with the words, "I will serve the Lord."

PRAYER: Lord, we praise you for giving us courage and strength to serve you every day. In Jesus' name, amen.